Look
After Yourself
Healthy
Food

Angela Royston

Heinemann
LIBRARY

www.heinemann.co.uk/library
Visit our website to find out more information about **Heinemann Library** books.

To order:
☎ Phone 44 (0) 1865 888066
🖹 Send a fax to 44 (0) 1865 314091
🖳 Visit the Heinemann Bookshop at www.heinemann.co.uk/library to browse our catalogue and order online.

First published in Great Britain by Heinemann Library, Halley Court, Jordan Hill, Oxford OX2 8EJ, part of Harcourt Education.
Heinemann is a registered trademark of Harcourt Education Ltd.

© Harcourt Education Ltd 2003
First published in paperback in 2004
The moral right of the proprietor has been asserted.

Editorial: Sarah Eason and Kathy Peltan
Design: Dave Oakley, Arnos Design
Picture Research: Helen Reilly, Arnos Design
Production: Edward Moore

Originated by Dot Gradations Ltd
Printed and bound in Hong Kong and China by South China

ISBN 0 431 18019 9 (hardback)
07 06 05 04 03
10 9 8 7 6 5 4 3 2 1

ISBN 0 431 18029 6 (paperback)
08 07 06 05 04
10 9 8 7 6 5 4 3 2 1

British Library Cataloguing in Publication Data
Royston, Angela
Healthy food. – (Look after yourself)
1.Nutrition – Juvenile literature
I.Title
613.2

A full catalogue record for this book is available from the British Library.

Acknowledgements
The publishers would like to thank the following for permission to reproduce photographs: Bubbles p.**23** (Claire Paxton); Corbis p.**13**; Photodisc pp.**11**, **12**, **18**, **22**; Powerstock p.**20**; Science Photo Library p.**26**; Trevor Clifford pp.**4**, **5**, **6**, **7**, **9**, **14**, **15**, **16**, **17**, **21**, **24**, **27**; Trip p.**8** (S. Grant), p.**19** (Zarember), p.**25** (Chester).

Cover photograph reproduced with permission of Zefa/BP/Hein Van den Heuvel.

The publishers would like to thank David Wright for his assistance in the preparation of this book.

Every effort has been made to contact copyright holders of any material reproduced in this book. Any omissions will be rectified in subsequent printings if notice is given to the publishers.

Contents

Words written in bold, **like this**, are explained in the Glossary.

Your body

Your body is like a complicated machine.
Most machines need fuel to keep them going.
Car engines burn petrol to make them work.
Food is your body's fuel.

Your body uses food to make energy. This book is about food. It shows how different kinds of food are needed to keep your body machine going.

Eating

Before your body can use food, the food has to be broken down into tiny pieces. Your teeth, tongue and mouth chew food into small pieces.

When you swallow, you push food down into your **stomach**. Here the food is broken down into even smaller pieces that your body can use.

Eat a variety of foods

It is good to eat food that you enjoy, but make sure you eat a large range of foods. Different kinds of food help your body in different ways.

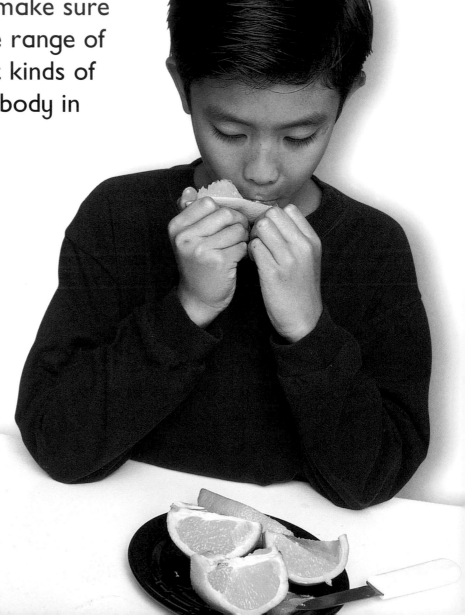

If you never eat fruit or vegetables, for example, your body will not work so well. Eating many different kinds of food keeps your body healthy.

A balance of good health

To keep healthy you need to eat more of some kinds of food than of others. Here are the different kinds of food you probably eat every day.

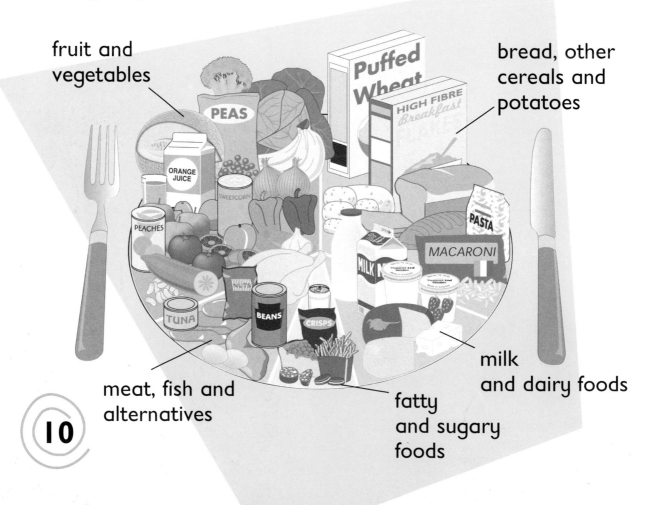

fruit and vegetables

bread, other cereals and potatoes

meat, fish and alternatives

fatty and sugary foods

milk and dairy foods

You should eat three meals a day: one when you get up, another in the middle of the day and a third in the evening. This will give you enough energy to last you all day.

Eat plenty of starchy food

These foods are all full of **starch**. Starch gives you energy. Make sure you eat one or more of this kind of food at every meal.

Your body uses energy all the time. When you run about, your muscles use lots of energy. But even sitting still uses energy.

Eat plenty of fruit and vegetables

Fruit and vegetables contain lots of **vitamins** and **minerals**. These substances help your body to work properly. Other foods contain some vitamins and minerals, too.

Each vitamin and mineral helps your body in a different way. Some minerals make your bones strong. Some vitamins make your skin healthy.

Eat enough fibre

Fruit and vegetables contain something called **fibre**. Jacket potatoes, **wholemeal** bread and other wholemeal foods contain fibre, too. This sandwich has lots of fibre.

Fibre is the parts of food that go right through your body. Fibre helps your body to get rid of waste food when you go to the toilet.

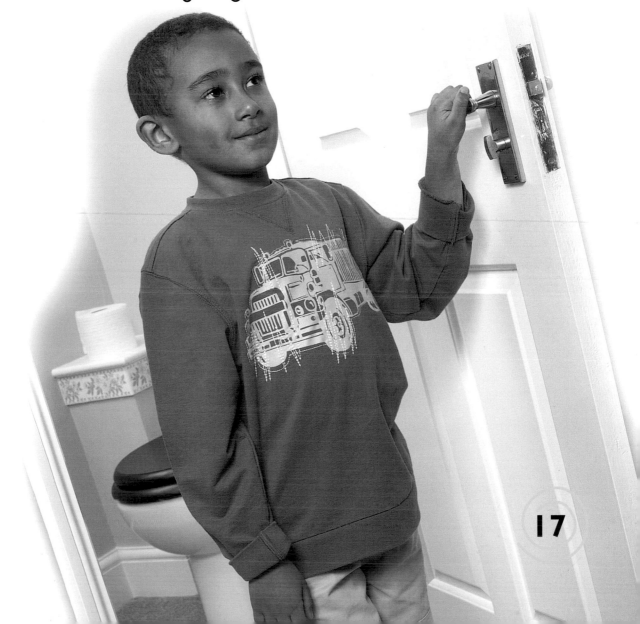

Foods that help you grow

These foods all contain a lot of **protein**. You should eat one or two portions of this kind of food every day. Most **starchy** foods contain some protein, too.

eggs

fish

beans

nuts

meat

Every part of your body is made
mainly of protein. You need to
eat protein in food to help
your body
grow bigger
and taller.

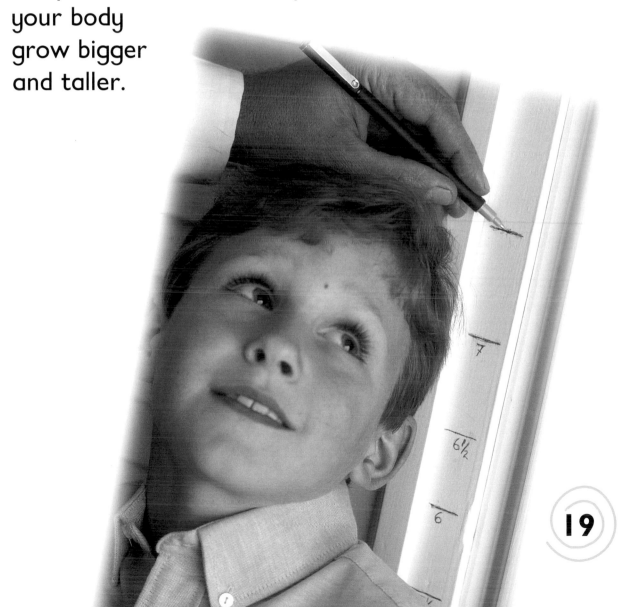

Drink plenty of milk

Milk contains a **mineral** called **calcium**. This mineral makes your bones and teeth strong and hard. You should drink milk every day.

20

All of these cheeses and yoghurts contain calcium, too. Some of them are made from cows' milk. Others are made from goats' milk or sheep's milk.

Avoid eating too much fat

These foods all contain a lot of fat. Fat gives you energy, like **starch** does. But just a small amount of fat gives you a lot of energy.

Your body also uses fat to keep you warm.
It stores extra fat in a layer under your skin.
If you eat too much you will store too much
and get fat.

Sugar attacks your teeth

These drinks and foods all contain a lot of sugar. Sugar tastes sweet and gives you energy. But do not eat or drink too much sugar.

24

When you eat or drink sweet things, some sugar is left in your mouth. This sugar can damage your teeth. Try to clean your teeth after eating or drinking anything sweet.

Drink plenty of water

You need to drink lots of water to stay healthy. Your body loses water in **sweat** and when you pee.

You need to drink about five or six cups of liquid a day to replace the water you lose. All drinks are mainly water. Food also contains water. Choose drinks that are not sweet, and drink lots of plain water, too.

It's a fact!

Some people are allergic to certain foods. This means that when they eat them their body reacts as if they are ill. They may be sick, their mouth may swell up, or they may get a rash on their skin.

People who are allergic to cows' milk can drink soya milk or goats' milk instead. They can also get **calcium** by eating **okra**, **watercress**, **sardines** or white bread.

The healthiest drink is clean water. Water helps your body to digest food. Drinking some milk and pure fruit juice is also good for your body, because they contain **vitamins** and **minerals**.

Sweet drinks are bad for your teeth. Sweet drinks include lemonade, cola and fruit squash or cordial.

Eating or drinking sugary things will give you a quick burst of energy, but the energy does not last. Soon you feel more tired than before you had the sugar. The energy you get from eating **starch** lasts much longer.

You can live for over a week without food, but for only a few days without water.

Your **stomach** stores food for up to four hours.

Waste food can take more than a whole day and night to pass through your body.

Glossary

calcium   mineral that makes your teeth and bones strong and hard

fibre   parts of plants that the body cannot digest and that pass right through the body

mineral   chemical that is found in some foods and that your body needs to stay healthy

okra   vegetable that consists of a sticky green pod

protein   chemicals in food that help your body to grow

sardine   sea fish, rather like a small herring

starch   substance that gives the body energy. Bread, potatoes and rice are all mainly made of starch.

stomach   part of the body into which your food goes when you have swallowed it

sweat   salty water that the body makes in the skin, particularly when you are too hot

vitamin   chemical that is found in some foods and that your body needs to stay healthy

watercress   plant that can be used in salads and soups

wholemeal   includes the fibre made from whole grains of wheat

Find out more

Body in Action: Eating by Claire Llewellyn (Black, 2003)

Eating Right by Elizabeth Vogel (PowerKids Press, 2001)

First Look at Diet and Health by Pat Thomas and Lesley Harker (Hodder Wayland, 2001)

My Healthy Body: Eating by Veronica Ross (Belitha Press, 2002)

Safe and Sound: Healthy Body by Angela Royston (Heinemann Library, 2000)

Shooting Stars: Healthy Habits by Rosie McCormick (Belitha Press, 2002)

Index